Bearing Up:

Teddy Bears as Catalysts in Caring Relationships

by

Florence Cranshaw

ISBN 0-932796-80-X

Library of Congress Catalog Card No. 97-60035

Printing (Last Digit)

6   5   4   3   2   1

Publisher—

Educational Media Corporation®

P.O. Box 21311

Minneapolis, MN 55421-0311

(612) 781-0088

Production editor—

Don L. Sorenson

Graphic designer—

Earl Sorenson

Artist—

Judith C. Grassia

Dedication

This book is dedicated to all peer helping groups, everywhere, but especially to my most important and supportive helping group— Cranny, Rick, Annie, Kate, Judy, Tom, Susie, Joe, Linda, John, Missy, Meaghann, Jeff, Ann, Vicki, Randy, Danielle, Peter, Terry and Laurel. I love you all.

About the Author

Florence Cranshaw has been a high school teacher, guidance counselor, counselor educator and peer helping trainer. Although retired since 1988 from the Dover Sherborn Schools, she has continued her activities in training peer groups and consulting with guidance programs in numerous schools in and around Boston. She is one of the founders of the Massachusetts Peer Helpers' Association, is active on their Board of Directors and on the Board of Directors of the National Peer Helpers Association. She and her husband live in Sherborn, Massachusetts, where they are in close touch with their six children, four children-in-law, and eight grandchildren.

Table of Contents

Acknowledgments

To recognize and thank the hundreds of people who made this book possible is well beyond the scope of these pages and my capabilities. Although I undertook the process of telling the stories, many of the ideas, the words, the concepts, the stories themselves, came from brains other than mine.

They came from the lively imaginations of dozens of students in the high schools and middle schools where I have been privileged to work. Zach Galvin and Rachel Derian, both graduates of Dover Sherborn High School, have to be at the very top of that list.

They came from counselors, teachers, and fellow members of the Massachusetts Peer Helpers' Association who provided complete stories or small vignettes—Linda Parker, Pauline Finberg, Judy Whittemore, Carolyn Kelley and my colleague and friend Thom Hughart.

They came from family members—Judy and Tom Grassia, Linda Parker, Rick Cranshaw, my husband Harold (Cranny), and my niece Anne Cranshaw.

I am indebted to Dr. V. Alex Kehayan of Edu-Psych, Inc., in Ridgewood, New Jersey for enabling me to clarify murky areas in times and spaces.

I am particularly and forever grateful to Joan Sturkie of Sturkie Services for Peer Programs in Longview, Texas, for her friendship, her warm support and genuine enthusiasm for my project, her foreword, her great care and patience in reading and re-reading my manuscript and for all of her helpful suggestions for change.

Foreword

Back in 1902 when a storekeeper in Brooklyn, New York placed two little handmade stuffed bears in his store window, how could anyone have known that 90 years later the world would be saying, "We love Teddy Bears." Yes, Mr. and Mrs. Morris Michtom, the storekeeper and his bear-making wife, really started something! And all because a cartoonist had placed a drawing in a newspaper referring to an incident when President Teddy Roosevelt refused to shoot a captured bear. We are indebted to Mr. and Mrs. Michtom, as well as the Steiff Company in Germany who started making stuffed bears about the same time, for giving the world the first "Teddy Bears." Where would we be without them?

This book is about those lovable little bears. It is also about human beings, and the caring that is shown one to another. However, expressing caring is sometimes difficult, even though it is genuinely felt. Often times, we want to reach out to someone, but we are reluctant because we don't quite know how to go about it. That is when "Teddy" can save the day. With wonderful stories from real life experiences, Florence Cranshaw shows us how effective a little stuffed bear can be.

Unlike many of us humans who prefer working with a certain age group, Teddy's expertise crosses all age groups. He has been used in hospitals and police stations to comfort children in crisis. School age children, elementary through college, have found him invaluable in peer counseling and peer helping classes. Adults in support groups and training sessions have worked out problems with the help of Teddy. Senior citizens have used him in peer counseling in their centers.

This book shows us the various places where Teddy can be used, but the main emphasis is on the school campus in a peer counseling setting. It reassures even the most skeptical that young people are willing and able to accomplish great things. Teddy is an ally in the pursuit of those goals.

Like Florence Cranshaw, I too worked with young people in a high school peer counseling class. My classes used Teddy in a different way than Florence's did, but that precisely is what makes Teddy so valuable. He is flexible (no pun intended). He can be used in many different ways by various people in a variety of settings.

Before my peer counseling days, I had no idea what a profound impact a stuffed animal could make on a group of students. However, when former students away at college began to write back and ask me about Teddy, I knew his influence was even greater than I had realized. One simple exercise using one stuffed bear had made a lasting memory. Now I find Teddy makes the same impression with adults in workshop settings. Each time I pack my suitcase to travel to a new location, Teddy goes right along. I can honestly say, I can never remember doing a workshop without Teddy.

I was elated when Florence Cranshaw told me she was doing a book on bears. When I read the book I was ecstatic. She had captured in words all the wonderful things I had experienced with bears all these many years. And who better than Florence Cranshaw to do just that! In fact, when I think of the adjectives to describe Teddy, I think of the same ones to describe Florence. Teddy is approachable, flexible, nonjudgmental, consistent (never moody), lovable, huggable; he keeps confidences, spreads good cheer, and keeps going year after year. That's Teddy and that's Florence.

When I read this book, I laughed, I cried, and I learned. The people in the stories are brought to life, and their situations become real. I don't believe anyone can read this book without being entertained, emotionally moved, and, yes, even humbled. How can we help but be humbled when we realize what a little stuffed animal can do. After all it is only a bear. But what a bear! Thank you Mr. and Mrs. Morris Michtom for bringing us a bear. And thank you Florence Cranshaw for bringing that bear to life on the pages of this book.

Joan Sturkie

Introduction

Teddy Bear: Originally, a child's stuffed toy, soft and cuddly, named after Teddy Roosevelt, who was depicted in a cartoon as refusing to shoot a small captive bear as a trophy for his hunt. Now a popular collector's item, with individual bear artists and manufacturers creating and producing hundreds of new designs each year.

Peer Counseling, Peer Helping: Programs that teach the skills of listening, caring, and reaching out to help other people, usually but not exclusively within the same peer group. Most often found in high school settings, but rapidly moving into other levels in schools as well as in industry and other institutions.

It was at the First Annual Conference of the National Peer Helpers Association at Lindenwood College in St. Charles, Missouri, in mid-June of 1987, that two of my great passions—Teddy Bears and peer helping—came together for me. Someone else made the connection and I am forever indebted to her.

In the closing session of the conference, participants were asked to make brief comments about special activities or ideas from their programs—much like a mini-share shop. There were many exciting ideas voiced at the time, but all are eclipsed from my memory by Joan Sturkie, who stood to tell us about a stuffed bear that she used with her peers in their program. I think I remember that she held the bear over her head as she spoke, but that could be just one more product of my imagination, which often clicks in, full bore, to serve me when my memory goes along its impatient way.

The bear, she said, was used on special occasions in her training groups. "Doing the Teddy Bear" meant passing the bear from one person to another as they sat in the circle. She would usually start the process, choosing someone to whom she wanted to give a special message. It might be someone who was having a difficult time at home or in school or someone she thought deserved an extra pat on the back because he or she had done something special. Then the bear would be given by that person to someone else in the group, and on to another and another, until each individual had received the bear at least once. Giving and receiving the bear gave everyone the opportunity and the permission to voice with honesty their love and appreciation for other members of the group. It opened the minds of the students to the value of verbalizing their positive feelings about each other. "Doing the bear" had become a treasured activity in the peer counseling classes, and was described later in her book (Sturkie, 1987), *Listening With Love: True Stories from Peer Counseling.*

What a great idea!

Our Peer Counseling Program at Dover Sherborn High School in Dover, Massachusetts, had been in existence since 1976. My colleague Thom Hughart and I, unaware of similar programs elsewhere, had developed strategies for teaching the art of helping to high school students. Knowing that in times of stress they first turned to each other, and hoping to tap into this vast resource of potential help, we devised activities and lessons to teach them listening and responding, problem solving and decision making. We were ecstatic with the success of the program, elated by the enthusiasm of the students, and amazed at their competence and energy. Peer counseling *worked!*

It took a little longer to win the enthusiasm of other professionals. Not everyone was convinced that kids could "counsel" other kids. It was not until we had struggled through our beginning years that information about programs in Florida and California began to seep through to us. We were not alone.

Unknown to us, Peer Helping had become a viable concept elsewhere in the United States. The organization of the National Peer Helpers Association and the occasion of that First Annual Conference was a thrilling boost to a dream of seeing the implementation of peer programs state and nationwide. Meeting talented, energetic, dedicated professionals from all over the United States was a peak experience of the highest order. And the idea of using Teddy Bears in our program was right up my alley.

Why should it be so hard to show our friends, acquaintances, co-workers, people in general, how much we appreciate them, like them, even love them, when the results are so unbelievably rich and rewarding, we wondered. Using Teddy Bears to make it easier was a new and wonderful concept. It might even afford us the opportunity of showing our concern or appreciation for someone outside the group. Why not?

Here was something that might bring comfort to persons who were hurt or confused, sad, lonely or alone. It could tell individuals that they were being perceived as worthwhile, that they were *not* alone, that some people did care about what they did and about what was happening to them. Above all, it could help to heighten the sensitivity of the students to the situations and the feelings of those around them. This was something that we *had* to do in our peer program.

We began the following school year, and quickly expanded our giving to persons outside the group. It became a treasured time for us as well, and as students and their advisors learned about it, "doing the bears" became popular in other schools in the area. It has been an incredibly moving, powerful activity—for the peer helpers, their friends, their families and their schools.

It is hardly surprising that many heartwarming moments have been experienced by those of us who have introduced Teddy Bears to our peer helping programs. Some are recorded here.

But this book is not just a collection of charming bear stories. It is a small sample of stories that for me, tug away at the negative impressions about teenagers so often expressed by adults. In the face of daily tales of violence and crime, of youthful drug and alcohol abuse, it is easy to succumb to the generalized concept of peer pressure in a negative sense—we rarely hear the stories that would help us to understand the entire, more wholesome picture of our young people.

Teddy Bears in these caring young hands give them a vehicle for demonstrating their marvelous strength and sensitivity, their capacity for goodness, kindness and warmth, their love for each other, and their intense need to love and be loved.

They too are not alone. Numerous reports of Teddy Bears being used as gifts of solace or celebrations of joy can be found in the adult population worldwide. I have included brief summaries of just a few of these, because they are important to me. They help me to believe, in spite of the terrors and miseries that surround us and are reported to us every day, that there is love and decency and goodness around us as well—that there is hope for us all.

And I am comforted.

To prevent any embarrassment to the people involved, a few identifying facts have been altered slightly in some of the stories, and in most instances I have changed the names of the bear recipients. None of the peer discussions are verbatim reports. All conversations are reconstructed from my own memory, or from the memory of those who relayed their stories to me. Any omissions or misconstructions are totally my own.

Chapter 1

In the Beginning

"Are you busy? Can I see you for just a minute, Mrs. C?"

"Sure, come on in, Cathy. How are you, anyway? What's up?"

"Oh, I'm okay, Mrs. C., but I was just wondering.... I mean, I know you don't talk to other people about stuff kids tell you, but is it okay for me to talk to you about somebody else?"

"Well, you know it stays in here unless there's some danger of somebody getting hurt if we don't tell, Cathy. And you don't have to give me names to begin with if that would make it easier. What's the trouble?"

"Ummm, it's like, some kids I know are really having some problems, and they don't want to talk to anybody in guidance. At least, not yet. And it's not like they were doing anything wrong, but they sure do have problems, and maybe they *could* get into trouble and I don't know how to help them."

"Are you saying you want me to help them, but you don't know how to get them to come here and talk to me?"

"Well, sort of.... But no, not really, though. I guess I was just like wondering if you could tell me what to do next if you knew the problems, and then maybe I could help, and I wouldn't do anything stupid."

"What kind of problems are we talking about, Cathy?"

"See, it's like, I'm an aide in the Freshmen Phys. Ed. class, and some of the younger kids talk to me in the locker room, and they have all kinds of questions about dating and, well, sex. I know they've all had tons of stuff about that in health classes since day one, but they haven't *really* had the firsthand experience of heavy dating pressure and don't know how to handle it. They hear all kinds of stories, some of them are even true, and well, they're really mixed up. Some of them have sisters in the Junior High and they're asking questions too. You see what I mean?"

"Mrs. C., can I talk to you for a minute? It won't take long, and it's really important."

"Oh, hi, Liz. Come on in. Just let me put these papers where I'll be able to find them the next time I'm hunting for them. So, what's happening? Are you okay?"

"Oh, sure, I'm fine—great, as a matter of fact. Aced that Calculus test I was sweating over. No it's not about me—it's one of my friends, or really, a friend of a friend, and her parents are going through a divorce, and she's really hurting about it, and nobody knows how to help. Actually, I know several kids whose parents are splitting up, and it's real hard to know what to say or do, and it's worse not saying anything at all to them. It's like not knowing what to say to somebody when someone in the family dies or something. Isn't there something we could do?"

 Educational Media Corporation®

"Good morning, Leeanne. I've been wondering how you made out the other day when you left to go to the new class. You didn't seem at all keen on the idea. How did it go?"

"Oh, that was fine, Mrs. C. Actually, I made this appointment to talk to you about something else. Remember the discussion we had in Mr. Davis' Psych class? We really started to talk pretty honestly about some things. It made me think of all the times when I was in the eighth grade, even the ninth, I guess, when I wished I had a chance to talk to somebody else about things that were bothering me. I don't know, maybe they were just little things, but it sure would have helped to be able to talk to *someone*. It wasn't stuff I would have brought to my guidance counselor, though."

"Do you mean you would have liked to talked to an adult and couldn't or...?"

"Well, no, not really—but all kinds of everyday things—not being liked by a boy I sort of liked, or never being sure whether the popular kids were going to like me, or wondering why a certain teacher never called on me when my hand was up—even more serious things like wondering if maybe I was adopted or gay or something like that. It turns out I wasn't either one, but you know what I mean? There were so many things to worry about."

My mind drifts back to the year 1971. I am a Guidance Counselor at Dover Sherborn High School. I am interested in groups and have some going in the Senior High School. They are going well. Some others in the Junior High are not going well—at all.

I wonder. What would happen if I mix them up? I decide to try it.

Instant group! Do these high school students have something I don't have?

Well, youth, for one thing—that gives them a lot—jargon, recent experiences in the Junior High—the very same building, teachers, busses, cliques, hassles.

But, how can I reach them if I'm not close to their age, closer to their experiences? Could I use the people who do fit that description—the students? Am I overlooking a terrific resource? How can I tap it?

I have put some of that early wondering on hold. On becoming Guidance Director in the following year, other issues temporarily occupy my time and energies. Although I continue to work with groups in the high school, I have relinquished my Junior High case load, and am in touch with student issues mainly through the Middle School guidance counselor.

Fortunately for me, a wonderful ally appears on the scene.

The Boards of Health of the two towns have had an active outreach program for the youth of Dover and Sherborn. At the retirement of the first director of the program, an energetic, caring young man is appointed to replace him. Thom Hughart has had a great deal of previous experience combating the serious problems of drug and alcohol abuse among young people. He is knowledgeable and compassionate, a skilled counselor. We find that we are compatible; we work well together.

Soon Thom verbalizes his concern that whatever he has done and is doing, it is never enough. I know the feeling.

"There's got to be a better way," he says. "It seems like I've been working with kids for a long time. I really wish I could be more effective. I've worked with some who have had drug and alcohol problems—lonely ones, bored ones—from bad or unhappy family situations. If only we could reach out to them before they get too hurt. If only we could get the other students—the ones who care and feel and see and hurt too. If we could only help them to help each other—boy, wouldn't that be something!"

A quiet bell rings in my head. We begin to talk about the possibilities.

"Could kids really counsel their peers? They talk together anyway."

"Could we devise a way of helping them to do that more effectively? Maybe we can work something out together."

"I think we could make it work. We'd have to put some time into planning, maybe lots of time."

"That's okay, but I'm sure glad there are two of us—to plan and co-lead. . ."

"Yeah, and keep the continuity when one of us has to be someplace else...."

"And use each other's brains and energies and skills..., and personalities, for that matter. We're really pretty different in a lot of ways."

"That will probably be a help, don't you think?"

"Sure it will. We'll need to lay out a whole year's worth of lesson plans and activities."

"And figure out a lot of 'what ifs'—I guess I mean build flexibility into it right from the start."

"Well, I'm ready. Let's do it!"

Dover Sherborn is like a lot of suburban high schools—it has its share of happy kids, serious kids, lonely kids, sad kids—and also a lot of students who really care about other people and are willing to put themselves to some trouble to help them when help is needed.

The high school and junior high school buildings are separate, but just across the athletic fields from each other—convenient geography for getting older students together with the seventh or eighth graders.

We spend a great deal of time during one spring and throughout the summer, planning and presenting our proposal to the high school principal, the teachers and the school committee. Finally, with the blessing of the administration and faculty, we begin our peer counseling program in the fall of 1976. Each year sees some modification of the program from the preceding year. With the unbelievably creative help of the students themselves, our program evolves and grows.

Although we allow for change and growth, there are some components that emerge as essential to the total program, and we do our best to incorporate them in the course of each year. We come to the conclusion that for us in training peer counselors, the basic principle should be helping the students in knowing themselves, accepting themselves, and then sharing parts of that self with others. This implies some lessons, exercises, or experiences about honesty, confidentiality, owning our feelings, making "I" statements, risk taking and trust. They learn the specific techniques of listening, responding, problem solving, getting started and closing.

We develop some special activities for helping students to become comfortable in giving each other positive feedback. We use the approach of Thanksgiving Day as a stepping stone to verbalizing our feelings of gratitude for the people who have in some way made a difference in our lives. Then, as the Christmas and Hanukkah holidays draw near, we go one step further. For our closing "party" before the vacation, we ask our students to look around the circle and to give verbal "gifts" to one another, in any order they wish. We have been part of the exhilarations, the tears, and the hugs that accompany this offering of admiration and trust, of acceptance of each other.

We soon discover that one of the hardest lessons for the students to learn is that helping or giving support does not equal giving advice. We use role plays, dyads, triads, fishbowl experiences, and lengthy discussions to help them see themselves more clearly, to begin to trust each other as allies in the helping business, and to build upon their repertoire of helping skills.

The students learn about using mutual interests through small talk to build rapport, about giving of themselves to establish a feeling of safety and trust, about setting goals for the counselor/counselee situation. Goals can range from dealing with sibling rivalry or family conflict, difficulties with particular teachers, making new friends, or even weight loss goals.

We find that one effective means of introducing our peer helpers to the younger students is to set up small discussion groups with junior high students.

They explore issues important to seventh and eighth graders—classes, teachers, peers, dances, and always the important questions of what it will be like for them in the high school—are the older kids really rough on freshmen? Do kids always get bullied in the lavs?

A natural extension of this visit to the junior high groups is the use of peer counselors in the orientation of students from the junior to the senior high school. They take eighth grade students in groups of 3 or 4 from their study halls and bring them to the high school for a tour of the building with small talk and questions on the way.

Students moving into the school during the summer are given an afternoon orientation by the Guidance Department before school begins, and we are assisted by the Peer Counselors in the same manner on this day. After hearing greetings from school personnel, they tour the building in very small groups and wind up over soft drinks and cookies. There they have a chance to help the new students get to know a few faces and places, to resolve a few confusions—when and where to catch the bus, how to try out for sports, where to go for help—who is who and what is what.

Students new to the community during the school year are assisted by the assignment of a peer counselor who helps them to find rooms and buses, introduces them to teachers and classmates, and makes sure that the first few days in the corridors and the cafeteria at lunch are not too bewildering or friendless.

Being involved in these simple ways apart from their classroom training helps them to become helping individuals. The work that they do is part of that training. They bring their experiences back to the group so that everyone shares in the successes and failures of each, and everyone gains from all of the experiences.

When they are finally assigned to individual cases, we encourage them to bring to the group some of the difficulties they encounter, and to use the group as a "brain" to give them support and supervision. Sometimes in free discussion, more often in role play, the students "supervise" the peer counselor in the work being done.

Our school year brings new beginnings, and unfortunately, endings. A big part of peer counselor training is learning how to say goodbye to a timeslot without saying goodbye to a friendship. Not only does the end of the year bring about the termination of their counseling assignments—it brings the termination of the group meetings. Through our training, we have become close. Each group has developed its own personality.

We ask for written statements of their impressions from each of the group members. They tell us that it works. It really works.

"My first impression of Peer Counseling was a bunch of nervous kids all trying to say something, but waiting for someone else to go first, and feeling a little uncomfortable and out of place."

"I was very shy and intimidated. I have to admit that first day I wondered if PC was really for me. I just thought I'd be helping other kids. I never thought I'd get help in the process."

"To tell you the truth, I can't think of a single thing that I've done in Peer Counseling that was not both fun and useful. The pure joy of coming together with the group to talk, share, and love has been remarkable. I look forward to their friendship and openness each time I set foot in the door because I know that nothing but good will come out of it."

"Our particular group has grown very close, and I can feel that bond among us. But the program is a lot more than a group of kids getting to know each other and counseling people. Most of all, I learned about myself and that eventually what we learn about ourselves can be used to help others."

"I have learned about the very special relationship of people helping people. It has proven to me how a little love, respect and caring can cure almost anything."

"I've found out how to really listen. It allows me to be quiet when I want and just listen to the conversation of the group."

"My view of the world has widened so incredibly in the past months. I can see how my whole perspective on life is continually changing and growing. And more importantly, that this is okay. There are no rules when it comes to feelings. What I have learned and shared here is something I will always treasure."

"It's become such a big part of me. It has helped me to explore deep inside myself to learn and discover feelings, wishes and dreams. It has taught me to share with others, to grow with others and to learn from those around me. To describe such a group as ours, I would say 'caring, understanding and honesty'."

"Deep down, I've learned it's okay to give myself a pat on the back when I know I've done my best."

"Living in the city and coming to a suburban school, I used to think everyone would exclude my thoughts and not respect them. But this class has proven that wrong. You've all given me a special gift that I hope will linger on for years to come—friendship. Thank you all for just being there."

"The nicest reward is the bond between me and my peer counselee—to be able to talk and care for another person is very special."

"I know now that I can go on and share with others with confidence and better understanding. Thank you all for taking me as I am, for being my friends, for taking my hand and sharing my cares. I love you all" (Cranshaw & Hughart, 1979).

Peer counseling works. It really works.

Surely, Teddy Bears will be given a warm welcome here.

Chapter 2

Only a Little Bear

"A *TEDDY BEAR*! Are you kidding?"

"Aww, cut it out Jeff; he's so cute!"

"Ooh! I just love bears. I've got a collection at home. He's littler than any of mine."

It is the beginning of the school year following the First Annual Conference of the National Peer Helpers Association. I am with the Peer Counseling II group. They began their training during the preceding school year, meeting

---

twice weekly throughout the school year, as they do now. They are learning new skills, more advanced strategies, and while continuing their one-on-one assignments, will help with a variety of activities and projects. If their schedules permit, some will continue their training during their senior year, as "PC III's," meeting just once weekly.

We are in my office at Dover Sherborn High School. It is a large pleasant space, but twelve students and two advisors do make for a cozy fit.

We don't mind at all.

In the school year preceding this meeting, they have asked for my permission to rearrange the office furniture to make more room for a proper circle. I approve of their arrangement. It is much better for all of my groups, and puts my desk against the wall where it cannot be a barrier in my individual meetings with students.

It has not taken long for students to understand that our group time is a time which is not to be interrupted. Phone calls are not relayed. Students are not permitted to knock on the door to see the counselor during this hour. Just before the holiday season in the second year of the program, one student presented a gift to the group. It is a handsomely finished sign.

The first person to arrive hangs the sign on the door.

It says to all who approach:

Group Meeting
Please Do Not Disturb

We enjoy our crowded privacy. We are safe in here.

I am listening to the immediate reactions of my proposal for using Teddy Bears in our program.

"Let me see! Can I hold him?"

"Look, Maddie! He's jointed! Even his head!"

"Mmmm. . . so soft."

"Gee, I remember my first 'fully jointed bear.' That was, like, a million years ago."

"*You* had a bear, Bill? Did parents give little boys bears way back then?"

"Yeah, I wouldn't let go of him for anything—until I started school, I think. He's still around someplace. I could find him if I wanted to."

"This one's so little; I can hold him all in one hand."

"I want to see, too. Pass him around, will you?"

My passion for bears had begun a few years before the First Annual NPHA Conference in St. Louis. My niece, Anne Cranshaw, had launched what turned out to be a very successful business as a bear artist, creating and producing bears for the rapidly growing population of Teddy Bear enthusiasts—the arctophiles—in this country and abroad. As luck would have it, I saw her the week following the conference and told her about my revelation. Could she tell me about some small bears that might be suitable? (I had already decided that for us, small was better than large, which I think has turned out to be a good idea.)

"As a matter of fact, I'll give you this one," she said, pulling a fuzzy brown, four inch jointed bear from her pocket. "It's a new design and I just finished him. I'll donate him to your program, if you like."

Would I like? Well! Needless to say, the Dover Sherborn Bear program was launched then and there, thanks to a great idea contributed at the NPHA conference and to the enthusiasm and generosity of my talented, warm hearted bear designing niece.

Ann's company is the E. Willoughby Bear Company, now located in Cape Elizabeth, Maine. She also teaches bear making, and I soon enjoyed taking one of her workshops to be able to do my own bears, not realizing then that a steady supply would be necessary as the program progressed.

The Dover Sherborn students adopt the E. Willoughby name for the bear we first use and either accidentally or on purpose, change the spelling to E. Willabee. From the first, E. Willabee is referred to as a male, also either accidentally or on purpose. To my knowledge, the decision is never challenged.

I describe the purpose and the process we will use with him. Although similar in concept, our bear program will be slightly different from that which had been described at the First NPHA Conference. On a weekly basis, in addition to our ongoing training, the students will discuss situations of which they have become aware, and come to their own decisions about who should have E. Willabee for the following week. They will also determine who is to deliver and retrieve the bear. In the beginning they might need to rehearse what they will say, but that will soon become a comfortable and possibly a sought-after task. At times there will be many candidates, and the talk will center around the order in which E. Willabee will travel—one week here, then on to the next person on the list, and the next, and so on. At other times, a unanimous decision may be arrived at in a matter of minutes.

To be honest, as I make the introduction of Ann's little bear, I am somewhat uncertain of the reception he will receive. There is no need to worry—he is an immediate hit. Everyone has to hold him, test his arms and legs and head, and welcome him into the group.

They plunge into the discussion of problems that might arise as he goes off to his first destination. As is usually the case once our trust in each other has been established, the students no longer look to us for clues as to what they "should" or "should not" say. Although they know we will plan an agenda for the day, we are just members of the group in our discussions, and the identity or role of the speaker is unimportant.

"Will people mind if they find out we've been talking about them in the group?"

"Won't they be embarrassed to know that we know about their personal problems?"

"I wouldn't be, but then, I'm used to sharing that stuff in here."

"But even if it was something nice, some people would be embarrassed to be told that it got noticed by other people."

"Well, yes and no. Some people might; others will probably like it. I would, I think."

"Won't they feel stupid having someone give them a Teddy Bear?"

"Yeah, just like a little kid."

"But Jeff, we don't have to give it to them in public, you know; we can always look for a way to talk to them in private, you know."

"No one is saying they have to carry him around like a comfort blanket."

"Why don't we give him to someone in the group for the first few weeks?"

"Hey, great, Amy! We could carry him around, maybe. Then other kids can see him around and get used to him."

"Hey, that's a good idea; let's do that!"

"Well, who then?"

Rachel tends to be one of our most insightful and articulate members. She notices things, and she often is one of the first to volunteer. Everyone listens when she speaks because they have come to value her honesty when she discusses her feelings and opinions.

"Well, I saw something that Chris did the other day that nobody seemed to notice," she said. "He helped a younger kid in a situation that other people would have ignored, and it couldn't have been easy under the circumstances. I don't want to go into detail, but you know what I'm talking about, don't you, Chris?"

Chris is a senior, a handsome, rugged six-foot-plus young man, co-captain of the basketball team, as much a leader in the athletic activities of our school as he is a leader in our program.

"Yeah, I know, and it wasn't really a big deal. But frankly, it's nice to know that someone thought it was special. Thanks, Rachel."

"Well, unless somebody has some other suggestions, I'd like Chris to be the first one to have E. Willabee. Chris is taking our goals in peer counseling right out where they need to be."

No one disagrees.

Chris walks out proudly at the end of the period, with E. Willabee peeking out of his shirt pocket. And that's where he keeps him all week.

E. Willabee is on his way.

In February of this school year, our Peer Counselors begin to prepare for the panel they will present at the First Annual Conference of the Massachusetts Peer Helpers' Association. With selected students from other high schools, they will discuss the activities they like best in their programs and they will talk about the activities or skill building they have found difficult.

For Chris and Rachel, the Dover Sherborn panelists, E. Willabee is first on the list of things they want to talk about. In their presentation, the bear is held up for display, and they tell of his travels, including his first visit to Chris.

The audience at most MPHA Conference presentations is urged to question and discuss, to participate and foster an interactive mood for each session. Questions come flying at the panelists.

They have a familiar ring.

"Aren't people embarrassed that you know about their personal problems?"

"Won't they feel stupid having someone give them a Teddy Bear?"

"What do they think when they find out you talked about them in the group?"

"Aren't some people embarrassed to be told they've done something nice that other people know about? I think I would be."

"He's so cute. Where can we get one like him?"

"How do you decide when there's more than one person suggested?"

And then the skeptic voice is heard-"A *TEDDY BEAR*! Are you kidding? You carried a *TEDDY BEAR* around for a *whole week*?"

At this, Chris smiles his beautiful smile, tucks E. Willabee back in his shirt pocket, gives him a little pat, and says, "Hey, guys, what's the big deal? He's only a *little* bear."

Chapter 3

Zack's Letter

Putting on conferences, especially first ones, is a nerve-wracking, mind-boggling, exhausting, frustrating, scary and harrowing task. They are a ride on a seesaw, a roller coaster, a risk-taking gamble. On the other hand, just like these, they often provide a huge gulp of fresh air, life-giving, revitalizing, exhilarating, energizing and thrilling.

Where will it be? How much will it cost? How much should we charge in order to pay the costs? Will anybody register? Will too many people register? How will we pay for the initial printing and mailings? How do we build a mailing list? Will we have enough room? Not enough food? Too much food? What if we have a major snowstorm? Will we have enough programs? Will the programs be well received? How will we know if they were well received? What do we do for openers? For closure?

The Committee for the First Annual Conference of the Massachusetts Peer Helpers Association experiences all of these emotions. They wrestle with all of these questions in addition to hundreds more as the date of the conference approaches.

The conference is held at Framingham State College in Framingham, Massachusetts on March 16, 1988, through the courtesy of the Office of Admissions and the kindness of Dr. Philip Dooher, Dean of Admissions. Arrangements are made quickly and easily. The College will be on Spring break; there will be no charge for the use of the facilities, we will deal directly with Food Services for the luncheon arrangements, which are reasonably priced.

Registration is flooded with applications. More than our maximum allowable numbers are received before the deadline—we turn them away. Money comes in quickly enough to repay individuals who have spent their own and for bills for printing and mailing. Labels are supplied on a one-time basis by our Massachusetts School Counselors Association. We have ample room. The food is great and plentiful. It does not storm but we have a code for calling the area radio and TV stations, just in case. Our programs promise to be exciting, the keynote speakers inspiring.

What to do for closing activities is no problem at all. This is what happens: the participants have been asked to complete evaluations of the sessions they have attended and of the entire conference; a tear-off section with names and addresses goes into a separate box to award door prizes during the closing activities. Since many of the members of the Conference Committee are well into "doing the Bears" by this time, it is decided that the door prizes will be small bears to enable other groups if they wish, to begin using them in the same way. Three names are called and the awards given. Dr. Dooher is thanked for his help and is given a much larger bear dressed in Framingham State colors. (This bear still resides in the office and is often re-outfitted by staff members who consider him a permanent part of the staff.)

Then Zack's letter from college is read.

"Hello, Mrs. C.,

"It's me—Zach! I'm just writing this letter to thank you for all you've ever given the kids and school through peer counseling. You really are something special and I thought long and hard about what you have shared with so many. Last night, an acquaintance of mine pushed his arm through a window and severed an artery and muscles to the bone of his upper arm. His girl friend, visiting for the weekend, was so incoherent and in such shock nobody could calm her down. They had both been drinking and the boy took out a problem on a window rather than his father who has an alcohol problem. Anyway, he went to the hospital and a friend of mine and I sat with his confused girlfriend for close to four hours. When I first saw the shocked, scared state she was in, I remembered what I had always done back at D.S. I ran down to my room, grabbed a comforter and my Teddy Bear, and ran back to the girl. She grabbed them both quickly and held on to them tightly for the entire evening. My friend and I talked with her and held her and listened to her until about 3:00 am this morning. By the time we suggested that she sleep for a while she had finally realized that her boyfriend's problem and accident were not her fault. She took the blanket and bear with her sleeping bag and quickly fell to sleep.

"I thought of you while I was lying in bed after the whole problem. Your E. Willabee has become a welcome friend even though he looks a little different. I guess any bear can be an E. Willabee.

"I guess what I'm trying to say to you is that I am really glad that I was one of you P.C. people. I'm beginning to realize that your ways and thoughts and techniques will be with me for a lifetime. Tom and you have really put a good thing in the school and anybody with doubts about it should be told otherwise. This year's P.C.'s should be told to pay close attention—they will use everything they talk about soon enough.

"Helping this total stranger and letting her know people were with her through the night with that bear really made me feel great. It was a great feeling of warmth and love and I must say, I owe it to you , Tom H., and everyone who ever put anything into peer counseling (including the bear). Well, I just wanted you to know that. . . . Stay healthy and happy.

Love and prayers, ZACH"

Chapter 4

The School Next Door

My office phone rings. It is the day following that first MPHA conference—just moments before our scheduled Peer Counseling II group meeting. Two of the students have already come in and have begun to rearrange the available chairs into our customary circle.

A counselor from one of our neighboring schools is calling. Their school is actually a powerful rival in every one of our varsity sports.

"Hi, it's me, Kathleen. My kids and I were at the conference yesterday and it was great, but we've got a problem here today. It's pretty urgent. I wonder if you can help."

"Well, what's up? What can I do?"

"I wondered if you have any more of those little bears that you talked about and gave away yesterday. We need one pretty badly."

"Gee, I don't have any more at the moment, but I can give you the phone number of my niece and I'm sure she'd get one to you pretty promptly."

I can hear the anxiety in her voice. "No, no, I really need one today. One of the girls in our group came home yesterday to the news that her sister had been killed in a car accident out where she was going to college. The kids want to have a bear for her. They're feeling pretty helpless. They really don't know what to do for her, but they remembered the bears from yesterday."

"That's so terrible. I'm just so sorry," I say. "We gave the last ones away at the conference. Let me get back to you as soon as I can. Our group is meeting in just a few minutes. I'll see what we can do."

The bell rings and the group bustles in, full of excitement about the preceding day. It takes a little longer than usual for everyone to settle in and "get focussed". Then I tell them about my telephone call, the tragedy for the girl and the problem for the peer group of one of our rival schools.

There is not one moment of hesitation. More than one voice responds, almost simultaneously, our rule of "One at a time" temporarily forgotten.

"What's wrong with giving them ours?"

"Give her E. Willabee!"

"Why not our E. Willabee?"

"Why not? That's great! How will we get him there?"

"I bet they can come get it, Mrs. C. Call them up. Tell them, right now."

No further encouragement is needed. I dial Kathleen and tell her that the group is meeting at this moment and they want to send E. Willabee to her group. Can she come, or should I find a way of getting the bear to her?

"Oh, that's so terrific. Thank them all for me and my group. I'll be there in ten minutes. Then someone can still take the bear to her today. Thank you, thank you. I'll be right there."

Several weeks later, a letter from the bereaved girl arrives at my office, addressed to the Dover Sherborn Peer Counselors. It is much more than a short "thank you for your expression of sympathy" note. She writes about the lift of spirits and the strength she has received from the presence of the bear during these weeks. She marvels at the caring that one group of young people who really do not know her have shown for her and her family. She will treasure the knowledge that students from a rival school had crossed over town line boundaries and rival school systems with love and warmth when it was badly needed. E. Willabee would be remembered as much more than a warm fuzzy.

Chapter 5

Bear Facts

In the first weeks after the introduction of the bear to our Peer Counselors at Dover Sherborn, E. Willabee has traveled the rounds inside the class, as the students themselves decide. Good deeds and successes are commended. The struggles and difficulties of our own lives are noted and our feelings made known. Expressions of honest admiration and words of comfort and caring gradually become easier. Our bear is helping in the growth of the group.

It is not long before it becomes time to send him outside the classroom.

E. Willabee will travel a great deal during the next few months, inside the group and outside. He visits with a student whose parents are going through a divorce. He goes home to someone whose boy-girl relationship has broken up. He visits a student whose grade expectations have been dashed, another who aces a dreaded exam, athletes whose teams have won or lost important games, someone whose dog has died, whose job has been lost.

---

*Some recipients take him home and keep him there.
Others carry him wherever they go. No one ever rejects him
or displays embarrassment in receiving him.*

Ms. Lombardo is a teacher beloved by many, students and teachers alike. Her drama and English classes are inspiring, and the plays and musicals she directs so awesome that it has become difficult to buy tickets before they are completely sold out.

The students persuade her to help us on our all-day workshop by spending a solid portion of the afternoon leading us through impromptu skits and awareness discussions. We persuade the administration to release her from her classes to be with us. We love every minute of it.

This is usually the day when the separate sections of the Peer Counseling program in our school come together, work together, learn new skills, and become better acquainted with everyone else. It brings together students new to the program with those who have had a year or more of training.

This particular day is also the first time that the new peers will give their bear to someone outside the group. They have been using their bear for a few weeks, using him inside their class—"PC 1" as it is dubbed—and will decide today where he will first travel away from them. A segment of time has been allotted toward the end of the day for them to make their decision while the other Peer Counseling classes—PC II and PC III (these students call their class PC III *Honor*)—hold brief meetings for their particular purposes. There is no contest. They can't wait to announce their choice.

"Ms. Lombardo, you have taught us so much, not just in your classes and plays, but most especially here today. You keep opening our eyes to our own feelings, and to how we come across to other people. You're so lively and creative and you care about kids a whole lot. We think our school is lucky to have you. *We* feel lucky to have you, and we want to thank you for taking the time to be with us today. It's been so much fun. You probably know about our bears. We'd like you to have the PC I bear for this next week, so you'll be reminded all week about how we feel about you."

"Did you guys know that Ms. Murray was in a serious car accident?"

"No, I didn't know. What happened?"

"She skidded on black ice on the way to school, I heard."

"Yeah; she was hurt too. I think it looked pretty bad. Somebody said they took her back to Boston in an ambulance, but I think she's okay. She wouldn't stay in the hospital; she's still home, though"

"And the car was totalled, too. That gorgeous car."

"Should we send a card?"

"Sure, good idea, Maddy. I'll get one and we can all sign it. Okay?"

"Hmm. Can we do it fast and send it to her at home? We don't know how soon she'll be back."

"I bet it won't be long. You know her. She's so intense about her classes."

"Yeah; she's tough, too."

"I think she's tough for a good reason. She really wants us to learn. It's not like it's just a job for her. I hope she does get back soon. No subs can do all she does in a day or two."

"Sounds like maybe she should have the bear when she comes back, for more than one reason. What do you think?"

"Do you think it would be okay to send E. Willabee to someone in the Junior High? I know we haven't done that before, and I'm not even sure I would know how to do it."

"Why, what's happening?"

"Well, you know my brother in the eighth grade—his best friend is really sick."

"What's wrong with him, Rob?"

"I'm not sure what the problem is, but it sounds pretty bad. He's already missed a ton of school. I feel sort of bad, because he's really a great little kid. He's been around the house a lot, you know, so I know him pretty well. But my brother is really bummed out about it."

"Are you saying that maybe we should give the bear to your brother, or what?"

"Now that you mention it, I hadn't thought about giving it to my brother, you know, only to his friend."

"Hey, I know what! How about you give the bear to your brother, and *he* gives the bear to his friend? Would your brother know what to say?"

"No problem. I'll coach him if I have to. Could we do that?"

"That's terrific! That way you get to let your brother know we're sorry about his friend, and then that gives *him* a chance to let his friend know how he's feeling. Let's do it. Okay, everybody?"

I arrive at school one morning to the shocking news that one of our teachers has died of a heart attack while jogging an hour earlier. The staff does not yet know. The students have no way of knowing either. It is the beginning of a sad and difficult number of days and weeks.

E. Willabee and PC I Bear spend the next two weeks in the Faculty Room.

In another school system, the plans for a major renovation of one of the older buildings call for a shifting of grades, classes, teachers and students. All of the complaints, major and minor, about the discomforts and inconvenience to students, teachers and parents seem to fall on the superintendent, over and above the problems of financing and implementation. The students take their bear to him. A letter comes to the group.

"You made my day and my week. . . . Thank you for letting me know that students care about their teachers and administrators. . . . Thank you for your concern, and thank you for the gift of yourselves."

In still another school, students sense that their *new* superintendent has his hands more than full. Perhaps he needs an encouraging pat on the back. Their bear goes to that Central Administration Office for a week.

Bear itineraries out into the communities of schools with peer helping programs seem to be a natural development.

Traumatic events are recognized.

The entire home of one family is destroyed by fire. Although there are no members of the family in the high school, the students take the bear to them.

And joyful events are celebrated.

A new baby arrives in the family of one peer helper. The group sends the bear to her mother.

Just a Teddy Bear. A small symbol of caring. A tool giving us permission to show compassion and love for one another, permission to be open and warm and nurturing, to show decency and kindness to anyone who is willing to see it, to let our real feelings and selves be visible to the world.

Chapter 6

Bear Coincidence

It is the year following my retirement as Guidance Director at Dover Sherborn High School. My fear of losing touch with young people has been eased by an invitation to do the training for a new Peer Counseling group with my colleague, Thom Hughart. We will be at Middlebury High School, a large suburban school near Cape Cod.

Space being at a premium as we begin our Peer Counselor program training, the resourceful and energetic Peer Advisor, Mr. Robert Desaulniers, Adjustment Counselor for the school, has liberated for us the stage of the school auditorium. Except for assemblies or large meetings, the auditorium and the stage are very available and quite private. Staff and students rarely come in without a spe-

cific program to attend. Being accustomed to meeting in classrooms or offices, the feeling engendered by looking out at the emptiness of row upon row of auditorium seats is at first somewhat eerie. In time, all of us have become accustomed to our given space, however. We have even begun to enjoy the easy availability of extra chairs and open space as we need them. We have grown as a group as well, and our focus has moved easily to what is happening within our circle, and just as easily enables us to ignore our unusual surroundings.

We are well along in the training program and have introduced the bear to the group some weeks before. Their bear has gone to other students as well as to teachers before this particular meeting, the meeting of the Great Bear Coincidence.

Society seems to have an inherent nervousness about coincidence, or at least some reservations about tales of coincidental happenings. Then again, any number of individuals have reported experiences which they claim to be true, but which try the imagination of the listener or reader, as the case may be.

The Great Bear Coincidence is experienced during this meeting, not just by me, but by my colleague Thom Hughart, the two program advisors and the entire team of Peer Helpers of Middlebury High School.

We begin the meeting, as has become our custom, by listening to the report of those who have delivered and retrieved the bear during the preceding week. One of the students, Ann, tells us that E. Willabee has visited the teacher they had agreed upon. He had been well received and warmly appreciated.

So, where is he at this moment?

"Oh, he's in my locker. I didn't have time to pick him up before coming here. Is it okay if I go get him right now? I'll only be a minute." And off she went, permission granted.

While waiting for the return of Ann and E. Willabee, the rest of the group resumes the conversation about his next destination. It seems that virtually all of the students know about yet another teacher, whose husband is seriously ill. She has been clearly distraught, and has been out of school to care for him for several days. A unanimous decision is made to give her the bear for the following week. Who will present the bear to her? What will they say? Is she back in school? Who will be able to find her quickly, preferably today?

The teacher, Ms. Green, they report, is back in school. One student has already had her class and now will not see her until tomorrow. Others only see her in Homeroom Period, which is over for today. Two will see her later in the day, but wonder about finding a private time to talk to her. They will look for a good time, perhaps right after class.

Just as the decision is completed, the left rear door of the auditorium opens and Ann comes in, holding E. Willabee up for us to see.

She has barely advanced ten feet down the aisle, when the *right* rear door opens, and in comes—Ms. Green!

An anxious and hushed exchange begins as Ms. Green proceeds down the aisle.

"It's her!"

"That's her!"

"What should we do?"

"What should we say?"

"Should we give it to her now?"

"Should we call her up here?"

Suddenly Ms. Green stops, perhaps recognizing the now muted tone of the group conversation. "I'm sorry, I didn't mean to interrupt. I didn't know you were in here. I'm just going through— it's sort of a short cut, you know," she adds apologetically.

No further guidance or instructions are necessary. Someone speaks up, one of the two who have agreed to present her with the bear. "No, no, Ms. Green. Come on up here and join us, please. Actually—we were just talking about you and we have something we want you to have."

Ann and Ms. Green approach the stage simultaneously, Ms. Green with a puzzled look on her face. Several students begin to speak.

"Mrs. Green, we know that your husband is sick, and that you're going through a difficult time right now."

"We want you to know that we're thinking about you, and we will all be thinking about you and him."

"We really hope he'll get better soon. We're sorry you're having such a bad time."

"We have this little bear. His name is E. Willabee, and we'd like to let you have him during this next week, so you'll know that we're thinking about you."

For a moment, Ms. Green just looks around at the circle of young and caring faces. Then she bursts into tears. The students descend on her with hugs and tears of their own. For a few moments, no conversation is possible. Then Ms. Green curls her fingers around E. Willabee, and holds him close to her face. She looks around the whole circle, meeting each set of eyes as she speaks.

"I *have* heard about your bear, but I guess I really didn't understand. I just didn't know or sense that students thought much about their teachers in a personal way, or knew or cared one way or the other about our problems. You don't know what this means to me—or maybe you do. Thank you, all of you, for caring about other people and for caring about me. I'll never forget this, or you."

She exits the auditorium, drying her eyes as she goes through the door.

Chapter 7

More Than One Bear

My retirement at times seems busier than my "work-ing" years. More Peer Programs are being implemented, and I am available, happily, to help with training in more than one school.

The peer program at West Bridgewater High School, southwest of Boston, has been in place for several years. Their advisor, a good friend and ardent supporter of the peer helping movement in Massachusetts, calls to ask if I would be willing to work with them for a short amount of time.

The West Bridgewater program has been successful to date. It had been introduced and implemented as a Peer Education Program, the main goals being to do workshops and presentations for younger students around critical issues for young people in the school and community. With high enthusiasm and energy they have devised and implemented a number of well-received activities. They are ready for more. But what?

Are there some strategies for injecting new life into the program, some new skills, new and different goals? Would I help? Of course.

Our first few meetings, predictably, are centered around getting to know each other. As in other programs, we use a variety of activities—dyads and triads, "fishbowl" sessions and lengthy discussions involving attitudes and opinions about important personal issues. They help us to learn the skills of listening and responding, problem solving, and decision making.

All of our meetings are based on three primary rules:

1. "One at a time"—the rule of respecting other people's right to say what they have to say.

2. "Using the personal pronoun 'I' instead of 'you' or 'people' or 'everybody' when it is appropriate to do so."

3. "What we say in here stays in here"—our rule of confidentiality.

We talk about our rules on a regular basis, having taken considerable time to explain the reasons for them at the beginning of the training. Remembering to speak one at a time teaches listening as well as respect for each other. Using the personal pronoun "I" helps to personalize our discussions. Most important of all, building trust in our group rests on the rule of confidentiality.

We talk often about the responsibilities involved in a confidential relationship, about the limits of that confidentiality and the need on the part of all of us to recognize our own limitations.

We stress over and over the dangers inherent in promising *never* to tell what we have heard. We stress understanding our responsibility in letting each other as well as any potential counselees know that we cannot keep secret any information that may do harm or endanger lives.

In this group at West Bridgewater, as in others, it is often the students who pick up on slight infractions. They have learned that they have been accepted genuinely by each other and by their advisors as worthwhile individuals. It is okay to remind each other that we are straying from any of our rules.

"Do you mean *you* don't like it when people say those things, Mike?"

"Well, yeah, you're right, I do mean, *I* don't like it when *anyone* says stuff like that."

Or, occasionally, on my part, arms spread out in some sort of restraining gesture, "Can we just hold on for a minute? It's hard to hear what everyone is trying to say. Okay, who was first? Who wants to start?"

They have learned that positive relationships with other people, including adults, are not only possible but hugely rewarding. Possibly because of this, we experience very few difficulties in these early sessions. They are eager to learn, to enhance the skills they have learned previously, to study and practice new skills, to devise new activities and projects with and for their fellow students, their school and their community. They are enthusiastic, dedicated, alike in many ways, and happily different in many others.

It is time to introduce the bear to them. Someone suggests immediately that, although in the group I am addressed as "Mrs. C.," the bear should be named after me—the Cranny Bear. She is passed around, duplicating an activity that is now very familiar to me. Again, everyone has to touch her fur, test her arms, legs and head, and try different positions. They approve.

Other problems do surface however, and quickly. Once again, they have a familiar ring. This time, in this group, the reservations so often voiced in the initial discussions about the bear are more intense. Two of the young men in the group are more persistent than the others in their objections.

"A *bear*! You can't be serious. That's for little kids," someone says.

Other students have other reactions.

"No, wait; it's more than that. It's about confidentiality with friends. We can talk all we want about confidentiality, but nobody's gonna believe us if we admit we've been talking about them to the rest of the group."

"Even if I know about somebody who has a problem, I'm not sure I would always want to talk about it, even here."

"I know I'll never be able to give the bear to anybody. They'd probably never trust me again."

A lively discussion follows. There is no need for me to intervene.

"But Rick, not every problem is a totally private problem."

"Yeah, that's the point. This is such a small school. Everybody knows everybody else's problems, or at least they think they know, and usually they don't have all the facts straight, either. It's a real pain."

Some of the young women are persistent, too.

"Well, what's wrong with letting other people know that we care that they have problems and are hurting?"

"I wouldn't want most people to know, that's for darned sure."

"Nobody will be forced to carry the bear around. They can keep it wherever they want."

"And what about the people who just do nice things? Lots of people never have any idea that anybody else appreciates them for what they do."

"Well, I guess I could buy into that, Heather—just don't even dream I would want to be the one to give him, I mean *her* (with a glance in my direction) to somebody else. I couldn't do it."

"What does that mean, then, Rick? Would you take part in deciding who gets the bear from week to week?"

"I guess it would depend on what we're talking about and who the person is. I still don't want to talk about some people or the things I know about that are too personal to them."

"Does that mean you don't trust us?" Now their persistence touches on a very sensitive issue.

"No, it's not that. I *might* talk about myself, maybe. I'm just not comfortable talking about other people if they have told me something they think I'm going to keep to myself."

"Well, I can relate to that."

"I can too. But we never *have* asked anybody to say anything in here that they didn't want to say, or share stuff they didn't want to."

"We don't even have to name the person we're talking about, do we, if we don't want to?"

The discussion goes on. Finally the decision is made for that week to have Cranny Bear visit a teacher who has been ill, who has only recently returned to school on a part time basis. Everyone agrees, including Rick, that this is a good place to start. Someone volunteers to deliver her. Cranny Bear is on her way.

Several weeks go by. The bear moves around from student to student to teacher and back, usually with little discussion as to candidates. There are enough visible hurts in the school to prevent difficulties of the type Rick has envisioned.

I am unsure. Are we missing some opportunities for offering our empathy where it might be needed and welcomed? We are certainly not in the business of invading anyone's privacy, but where does the need for privacy stop and dreadful loneliness and isolation begin? Have we been avoiding some of the more private and terrible pains out of deference to Rick's stated concerns about confidentiality? There is no way to know.

I arrive one morning to find the group assembled and solemn.

There has been a fatal accident over the weekend. The young man was not a student in the high school.

He was Rick's cousin.

They had grown up in the same house, just like brothers. They had been closer than brothers. What can anyone do?

This is not a time for a planned agenda. It is a time for learning about grieving, what to do or say for friends who have lost loved ones, about what might be helpful or not helpful. Most of all, it is a time for helping everyone to work through how each of them will respond to Rick right away and in the group when he returns to school. The latter proves to be the most difficult.

"He doesn't want to talk about it. I know," one of his closest friends says. There is no argument; no one knows Rick better. "I saw him last night. He won't talk to anybody, not even me."

"Are you saying we shouldn't say anything at all to him when he gets back?"

"I just know he won't want to talk about it."

"We can't just pretend nothing has happened. That wouldn't be right."

"Right. I know I'm going to feel real uncomfortable if we don't say anything to him at all."

"Well, what's more important, our feelings, or Rick's? If he doesn't want to talk about it, why should we be the ones to bring it up?"

"Well, most of us, I mean, *I'm* planning to go to the services. He can't help but know that everybody here knows."

"Actually, the whole school knows. Make that the whole town."

"Maybe we just have to wait until he's ready to talk about it."

"Could we just say we're sorry, like we just learned? At least that won't be phony, and he can respond if he wants to."

"That's a good idea. It's hard to know if he maybe wants to talk about it, but won't or maybe can't let himself be the first one to say anything."

"How about Cranny Bear? If anyone should have her next week, it should be him."

"Yeah, but you know how he feels about that."

"I wonder how he really feels."

"Was he just saying that he wouldn't want to be given the bear, or that he would be uncomfortable being the one who had to explain to anybody about why we thought *they* should have the bear?"

"Or maybe it was the idea of someone actually carrying the bear around for a week. He couldn't imagine anyone being comfortable with that. Or was he saying that *he* wouldn't be comfortable with that?"

"Well, we agreed that no one *had* to carry it around—only to give it to them to have for the week. I'm pretty sure he knows that."

"Wait, I have an idea." This is Rick's friend again. "I guess I pretty much felt the same as Rick about all this. But how about if I put the bear in his locker before he comes back? I know his combination because we store stuff for each other. Then he'll see the bear right away. That way he'll know we've been thinking about him without anybody having to say it. He can leave the bear right there if he wants to, but he'll know. If he wants, he could just return it to my locker before the next meeting, and he still won't have to say anything. But he'll know. He'll know," he repeats.

Rick does know. He returns the bear to his friend's locker at the end of the week of his return to school, without saying anything specific about it to anyone. He comes to our meeting in much his usual casual manner. But he is the first one to speak when we settle into our circle, which is not at all usual.

"I just want to thank you for the bear. It's hard for me to talk about all of this, so I just want to thank you all for letting me know that you were thinking about me. It was the best thing anybody could have done. Thanks."

Several weeks go by. Bear discussions have become more lively. More personal and private issues are being discussed, often accompanied by remarks about the privacy of the issue. But a trust base has been established—problems around confidentiality are never experienced. What we say in there stays in there.

One morning, reaching a bear decision begins to appear to be almost impossible. There are several candidates, all of their problems reported as being important and severe. The discussion is taking almost the entire period. Our agenda for training has been shoved aside. They can agree on delaying giving the bears for a week or two in some of the instances, but no decision can be reached about who should be the first.

Rick has gradually become a more active part of the debates. Now he speaks up, giving voice to his total conversion:

"I think we just need to have more than one bear."

Chapter 8

Katie Bear

The school year is coming to a close. In the West Bridgewater High School group, we have begun to evaluate the progress we have made toward our original goals and to define the next steps toward our long range ambitions. In the years that I have been working with peer counselors in various schools, hearing students talk about what they have learned, what they are proud of having accomplished, and listening to their awesome creative new ideas has always given me a tremendous rush of pleasure—one of the many rewards I have experienced often in peer helping work.

I arrive at school full of excitement in anticipation of our agenda for the day.

"We need to talk about something first," someone says as we pull chairs into our circle. I look around. Some of the girls are visibly upset.

Well, flexibility has always been a known and necessary ingredient. The students know that there is always a planned agenda for our meetings. They also know that important issues or crisis in their lives or in the school have priority over the agenda.

"Why, what's happening?"

The story tumbles out.

"You know there's this day care center down at the far end of the Middle School building, don't you?"

"Some of us go there on a regular basis as aides. It's part of our Family Living class—the child care part, you know."

"Well, there's this little girl, Katie. She got real sick all of a sudden and—it's so awful, but she *died* last night."

"We just heard about it this morning."

"Someone said it was meningitis."

"I can't believe she's gone. It was so fast."

"She was so adorable. I think she was only four years old."

No one says anything for a moment or two. Not everyone knows the little girl, but they can share in the grief of the ones who do. One of the girls who works in the center crosses the circle to sit next to another girl who is crying quietly. They sit and hug each other, while others murmur words of sympathy.

"I'm supposed to go over to the center today. I'm not sure I can handle it."

"Me neither. I'm so upset myself. I'm sure to make things worse for everybody. I can't imagine how the little kids feel."

"Will someone have told them already that she died? Who has to do that? I know I wouldn't want to. I just couldn't. I don't think I'd even want to be there when they do tell them."

"Those little kids might not even be able to understand that she isn't coming back. Isn't that possible, Mrs. C.?"

"It's very possible. Do you want to talk about what it will be like for you and for them when you do see them the first time?"

"I just don't know. How are they feeling? What do we say or do? I've never lost a close friend. And they're so *young!* Do we just say we're sorry that she's gone, and we'll miss her too?"

We sit in silence for a moment. Then someone says, "Well, would it be right to send the Cranny Bear to them?"

It gives us something to think about, maybe to do. We need something to do.

"Gee, I don't know. Do they know about our class, or anything about the bear?"

"Well, do they have to know anything about us? Is that necessary?"

"Would they understand what the bear was for?"

"Well, even if they didn't understand who we are or why we sent it, it might help if they had something cuddly to hold."

"But would children their age understand that it's only on loan for a week?"

"Maybe not. What do we do about that?"

"So, what's the difference? The year's almost over, and we can work on getting another bear by next year, can't we?"

"No problem. We'll think of something. But how do we deliver the bear?"

"I sure don't know. Anybody have any ideas?"

For a moment, no one responds. Then one of the girls who has been most visibly distressed speaks up for the first time.

"Just this once, could we ask somebody besides us to take the bear? I hate being a wimp, but I'd sure feel better if we didn't have to. I'm still not sure I could handle it."

"How about taking it to their teacher? I mean the ones who know her from being in the center? We could explain to her about the bear, and maybe she'd be willing to give it to them it for us. Even that will be hard enough."

"Great idea. She knows lots more about what to expect and what to do than we ever would. She'll be able to wait until she finds just the right time, too."

And so it is decided. Understanding our own limitations has been a frequent topic for discussion, and this certainly seems a good time to exercise that concept. Ownership of the bear is relinquished completely. It is sent as a permanent gift to the center, delivered to the teacher to be presented as she sees fit.

For the remainder of the school year and into the next, Katie Bear (as the toddlers rename her) has a special place on a low shelf in their classroom. If someone feels sad and wants to think about their friend Katie, Katie Bear can be held and cuddled. If someone just feels sad for any other reason, she is waiting to be picked up and stroked. She has a permanent home.

And the Peer Educators have a new bear the following September.

His name? Peer Ed.

Chapter 9

Mother Bear

E. Willabee continues to be known as E. Willabee in a number of schools. For these students, renaming him has never been an important issue. This is true in the Peer Counseling program at Medway High School, West of Boston. Their peer program has been in place for two and a half years, and E. Willabee has been a member of the group for more than a year.

As in other schools, finding destinations for the bear's weekly visits has never been difficult. Students have learned quickly that pain and suffering are everywhere; one only has to be aware of what is happening close by, to be sensitive to signals of distress and to listen attentively when someone talks about difficult personal issues or situations. They have learned too that every day many people

---

around them—teachers, administrators and students—are
performing acts of kindness that quite often are unnoticed
and unrewarded.

The group response has been beautiful. They use E. Willabee with enthusiasm, sending and retrieving him week after week to and from his errand of caring. They understand immediately that he is a symbol, not a substitute of that caring. In some instances, it is the best that they can do. Sometimes it is not enough, and they continue to search out ways to help, using the skills they have been practicing. They listen, they tutor, they befriend the lonely, they bring homework to students who are ill at home or in hospitals, they do workshops and projects.

In their meetings, they practice new skills, they discuss their individual and group activities and they wrestle with the weekly determination of E. Willabee's destination. It has become clear to them that problems come in all sizes and in too many places. They soon ask if it would be possible to have a second bear, and their counselor, Terri Campana, who is also a bear maker, provides one. He is not pocket sized like E. Willabee, being somewhat larger, nevertheless a comfortable small armful who nestles easily against cheeks or chests or shoulders. His jointed body is made of a soft warm beige and brown mohair. His large, slightly curled-over ears are "good for listening", the kids say. And the perky, quizzical expression on his face gives the impression of someone trying hard to understand. He is perfect for his job. To distinguish him in their discussions from E. Willabee, he becomes Bear Too. He begins to travel wherever he is needed.

Betsy is a Junior and a close friend of many of the peer counselors. She has suffered for many years with a serious gastric disorder and has missed a great deal of school for her frequent hospitalizations. It has been necessary for her to have at-home tutoring in order to continue with her education. Even when she is at home or on the rare occasions when she can attend school for a short amount of time, she is in constant pain. She is determined to graduate with her class, and works enthusiastically and doggedly with her tutors in spite of all the setbacks.

Betsy is often the focus of conversation in the group. The students are faithful companions, regular visitors to her home and the hospital, keeping her abreast of who is doing what in school, who is dating whom, what is happening of great or small significance, all helping her to feel connected with the day-to-day school life she cannot be a part of. She has been visited by E. Willabee on many occasions.

Now she is back in the hospital, facing further surgery.

"Betsy really needs a bear again this week."

"More surgery. It's pretty serious, too. They're doing a bunch of tests now."

"When does she have the operation? Maybe we should wait until it's over to give it to her."

"Yeah, maybe. But maybe she needs it more now before the surgery, while she's going through all those gruesome tests. That can't be any fun."

"I don't know how she keeps up her spirits the way she does."

"I don't think I've ever heard her complain, and I see her a lot."

"She worries more about her studies and grades than about being sick. I've seen her studying when she was so sick I wondered how she was holding her head up."

"And she's always worrying about her family, and the stress on everybody for her being sick, especially for her mother."

"Yeah, I'm at their house a lot. I know it's been hard on all of them. And you're right. It's been real hard for her mother, but you know, she's a lot like Betsy in that, or maybe Betsy's a lot like her mom, I guess. I've never ever heard her mother complain about the extra stress. I know how worried she is, but she just keeps on supporting Betsy, doing all the extra things that need to be done, cheering everybody else up. She's been super."

"No wonder Betsy's attitude is so great. She's had a good teacher."

"Hey, I have an idea. Why don't we take E. Willabee over to the hospital today so Betsy can have him before the operation, and then, could we maybe take Bear Too to Betsy's mother?"

"Cool idea."

"Why not?"

"Sounds like we all know she really deserves a pat on the back along with a warm fuzzy. What do you think, guys?"

No argument.

Bear Too goes to visit Betsy's mother.

Betsy's mother and family fall in love with him, and at the end of the week, can't "bear" to part with him. The group understands, and once again checks out the possibility of acquiring one more bear.

Bear Too is there in his new home with her family when Betsy returns from the hospital. She is able to graduate with her class, but Bear Too never comes back to school. He has already been graduated.

Chapter 10

Teacher Appreciation

A meeting is going on in the West Boylston High School PAL (Peers Are Listening) program. My daughter, Linda Parker, a special education teacher, has been the program advisor for this small west suburban high school for nine years. They have implemented the bear program early in that school year.

The students are trying to reach a decision about the bear nominee for the week. For some reason, in this first year of "doing the bears", they have often focussed on their teachers. At this moment, there are several teacher nominees.

"How about Mr. Thomas. You know, the Student Council Advisor. Maybe people just expected he'd do it, but he organized the whole Homecoming Week—I mean he did the whole thing, organized and did it! I can't even imagine all the work that was, and I don't think he *had* to do it, or anything. He just sort of does stuff like that—above and beyond, I think they call it."

"Yeah, well, that's cool all right, but I think we ought to consider Mrs. Johnson for the bear. You know, she's such a meanie lots of the time, maybe even most of the time. But, you know last week when Ms. Malloy fell and hurt herself so bad, Ms. Johnson was so unbelievable! She covered as many of Ms. Malloy's classes as she could, even doubled up some with her own. She was awesome. I just wouldn't have believed it if I hadn't seen it myself, and I know she volunteered to do it—it wasn't something she was ordered to do, you know."

Slowly gathering her courage, Holly, the quiet one in the group, begins to talk about her art teacher, Mrs. Tetler. She wants to nominate her for receiving the bear this week. Mrs. Tetler is a very popular teacher, a "neat lady" in the eyes of students as well as faculty.

"She's always been a pretty special teacher, but it's not that. And I know I'll need your help to do it. I'll have to sort of practice what to say to her, because I'm not sure how much she knows about the bear. I mean—she knows we *have* a bear and all that— most of the teachers do, I think—but see, it's sort of like. . . ."

"You don't have to tell us all the details if you don't want to, Holly," one of the peers puts in during the pause. "She is a neat person—I never heard anybody say anything but good things about her."

"No, it's really more than she's just a nice person and a good teacher—it's something specific that she did for me and it's okay; I do want you guys to know what it was."

"Okay, let's hear it then, but I already think it's a good idea, Holly."

"Well, see, I was in her class the other day, you know, but I was only there physically, if you know what I mean. I was having such a crummy day—I mean, totally crummy. And Ms. Tetler must have noticed, because she came up to me and asked me if I needed a little bit of time for myself. She was actually worried about me—not about the class work or anything—just about me. So she let me go for a little walk so I could get sorted out a little bit. I mean, it was just so nice knowing that she cared."

"That's really cool, Holly. I hope things got sorted out for you, though."

"I'm okay now. I'm really feeling much better, thanks. But you know, knowing that a teacher would do that for me helped a lot— I mean, having her notice I needed a break was as much help as *getting* the break. Anyway, that's why I'd like to let her have the bear this week."

Now Kathy, one of the more verbal students speaks up, supporting Holly and Ms. Tetler. "I'm with you, Holly—I don't think you ever nominated anyone before, and this seems pretty special—we all think she's special, anyway. So go for it."

Holly has just returned to class after giving the bear to Ms. Tetler.

"How did it go, Holly? What did you say?"

"And what did she say?"

"Well, I explained the purpose of the bear, like, some people got the bear because something pleasant has happened, or that the kids have seen some special efforts like hers to me, but others are given—or really loaned the bear because sadness or disappointment has entered their lives. I told her the bear was our way of recognizing the people behind the events."

"So what did she say?"

"She was really tickled to be nominated. She said it was like being inducted into a very special club, you know, as a member, because kids had nominated her for the award."

"Nice job, Holly. I'm really glad you suggested her."

It is a few weeks later, and Ms. Tetler has just stopped Ms. Parker in the corridor. She tells her that she was delighted and honored to receive the bear.

"Of course, I've seen the bear around school, and thought it was a nice thing for the kids to be doing. But having Holly explain it to me made me look at the whole activity.

"You know, I've been thinking about it a lot. It's really done something else for me, besides just being pleased about being nominated.

"Now I'm seeing other people around school with the bear, and when I do, it makes me watch that person with special eyes— I know that something significant is going on in their lives— something special has happened. Maybe I can help or recognize that person too!

"The other thing, Linda, about the bear, I mean, is that seeing the bear makes it easier for me to say something to that person— it's like an instant opener, and it's just not hard anymore to let the other person know that I'm thinking about them in their joy or sorrow or specialness. It's a pretty terrific thing to learn.

"And just think—I'm a teacher, and I learned it from kids."

Chapter 11

Breaking Through

"Look, this may seem sort of different to you guys, but I think Lisa should get the bear this week."

"Which Lisa?"

"You know, the Lisa that's in our gym class."

"Oh, cool; you're right. It's different, but I'm with you. She really should get it."

"Mrs. P., you know her too. She's in some of your classes. What do you think?"

"Well, yes, I do know who you mean, and I probably agree. But first tell me why you're suggesting her and why you think this is different. This is a group decision, don't forget."

Linda Parker is meeting with her PAL students at West Boylston High School. They are once again wrestling with the "bear" decision.

"Well, it's sort of hard to say and I hope it's okay to say it—actually, Lisa's a little different, I mean, she has lots of problems that make things hard for her that aren't hard for lots of other people."

"Yeah, but that's not why I suggested her—it's not because she's new and she has problems—it's because she helps us all—it's kind of hard to explain."

Lisa is in her second year in this high school; all of her previous education has been in substantially separate special education programs. Diagnosed in childhood as a high functioning autistic, she has been transferred in order to be mainstreamed into a regular school setting. Through the years, because of her high intelligence and perhaps because of the same determination observed by the peer counselors, she has shown considerable progress, overcoming one by one many of the barriers created by her personal social prison.

She struggles with all of the difficulties created by her ultra high sensitivity—touches that are painful to her skin, noises that are excruciating to her ears. Being in and near crowds—her fears of being touched by other people—had extended into an extreme possessiveness of her belongings—her schoolbags, books and pencils. She still has difficulty expressing herself; her language seems somehow mechanical and stilted; she still needs to be reminded from time to time to look at people when she speaks.

In spite of all of this, her incredible persistence is paying off. She no longer needs assistance to get to classes or to help her in the lunch line. She has gradually been assigned to several regular classrooms. In some areas, math, for instance, Lisa is beginning to excel. And the students are noticing. They have been rallying to help. They have seen for themselves that for her, communicating and connecting with other people is a critical issue. And a physical education class is a major problem.

"Wait, Jen—I think I sort of know what you mean. She tries so hard to do all the things that are pretty easy—or at least a lot easier for most of us. And it's even hard for her to let us help her, but she tries hard at that, too."

"Yeah, right. You can tell, I mean *I* can, that it's scary for her, but she just loves to learn, even when it's scary. And that's sort of what's so neat, that she accepts our help anyway, hard as it is, and we can see how proud she is for getting past that."

"And then *we* all feel so good that she's letting us help, and that it's helping her when we can help. I'm not sure I'm making any sense. Do you guys know what I mean?"

"It's really because she makes *us* feel good, not so much because she has problems. Is that what you mean? Because it's really true—she does make us feel good, just being with her. At least, she sure makes *me* feel good."

"But, when you think about it, it was sort of spooky—I think I was really a little afraid of her for a long time. Maybe that's why I was so surprised at feeling good about being with her."

"Me too. I think lots of us were. I didn't know how to talk to her at all at first. I guess if *she* was having problems relating to us, that was only half the problem. *I* sure didn't know how to relate to her."

"It's like Lisa has made us feel good getting over *our* problems in trying to communicate with her, and I don't think we're the only ones in the school that feel that way."

"You know, Mrs. P., you wouldn't *believe* the kids who are in that gym class—some I wouldn't have bet anything would ever get involved with helping other kids, and not just girls, either. I mean the guys too—some of the kids that want to act tough and hard, so careful not to show their emotions—you know, the macho ones—they're all into making sure that she gets as involved as she is able to. She just tries *so* hard at everything."

No one in the group has any reservations about Lisa's right to have the bear; the decision is unanimous and joyful. Now they begin to examine the next step—how to deliver and retrieve the bear.

"How will we explain it to her—I mean, why we're giving her our bear? Will she understand what it's all about even if we can come up with what we think is a good explanation?"

"Maybe she *won't* understand, but does it matter? I mean, is it really important for her to understand as long as she likes it?"

"Hey, maybe you're right. What difference does it make as long as it makes her feel good?"

"Okay, so maybe we won't worry about that. But what happens if she doesn't understand about giving it back at the end of the week, that it's like just on loan?"

"Oh, brother! That's even harder. I wouldn't know what to say."

"Neither would I, I don't think."

"Wait a minute. So what happens if she doesn't understand? The worst would be if we can't get the bear back. Then what?"

"Well, we'd just have to get another one somehow, wouldn't we?

"Can we, Mrs. Parker? Get another one, I mean, if we need to?"

The bear is delivered. A few minutes of role play helps the designated spokesperson, Jen, with the message for Lisa. The students write a note to accompany the verbal presentation. Lisa can check it over later, and if she wants, the staff can help her to understand. The script will say that people in class have noticed how hard she is working and that she makes other people feel good that she is there and it makes them all want to do well too and to help each other. It will explain that the bear is to tell her all week that she is helping others to feel good, and will remind her that she will have the bear for just one week; then the group wants to give it to the next person who has been nominated.

When the week is up, Lisa herself returns the bear to the main office, where the bear is known. The office secretary returns it to the group.

A determined young person, burdened with crucial uncertainties, has taught a large number of students and staff a major lesson in overcoming their own difficulties in relating to persons who are "different." And a small bear has relayed to her the gratitude of a sensitive group of her peers.

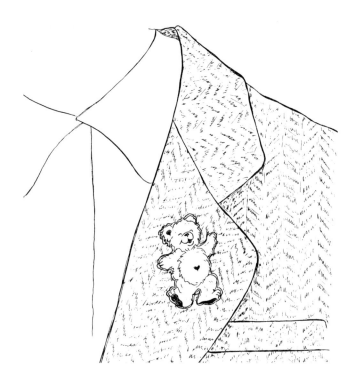

Chapter 12

Bearing Negotiations

We are planning one of the all-day training workshops that the Massachusetts Peer Helpers' Association offers to peer program advisors from time to time. It is hard to resist bringing bears into the agenda. Students have been consistently enthusiastic, but what will be the reception by adults, particularly if they are introduced to Teddy Bears at the end of just a single day's work together? Our instinct tells us to trust that caring adults who believe in peer helping will also embrace an idea that helps to demonstrate caring and empathy for other people.

But how can we possibly do only one bear, thus singling out one person from all the others?

We decide we can't do that. So, what do we do—give bears to everyone?

We decide we can't do that either—it is just not practical—not enough immediately available bears, and prohibitively expensive, too. But what can we do at the end of the day that will let each participant know that his or her efforts have been important, and how can we bring our bear concept into the process?

Someone remembers the book *Chicken Soup for the Soul.* In one story (Bridges, 1993), a teacher presented each of her students with ribbons imprinted with the words "Who I Am Makes a Difference." She told each one how he or she had made a difference to her and to her class. She then gave them each three more ribbons, with the assignment of going out to their community, their homes or their workplaces, honoring and acknowledging other people in the same way. They were to report on their activities in a week.

Just the thing. We will adapt this idea and modify it by using small fuzzy bear stickers as a substitute for ribbons or badges. Now we have a strategy involving bears that will enable us to give positive feedback to everyone in the group. We will give each person one sticker telling them how they have made a difference to the day's work, and send them out with more, to recognize and honor family or friends as they choose. At the same time, we will talk about "doing the bears" in other programs.

The bear stickers are accepted with as much enthusiasm as in any teenage group. Everyone leaves the workshop promising to carry them to new destinations, and if possible to let us know what happens.

Months later, one of the participants calls to tell us her story.

"It's been such a miserable year, I mean really miserable. I know we're not the only school to be in this situation, but we've been working without a contract all year, and the negotiating team has met time and again, only to be stalled over and over. It's just awful.

"Well, one of my good friends, Carol, is on the negotiating team, and she's been really having a terrible time with it. She's an English teacher, and we're really good friends, so I know there's a lot of stuff in her personal life that's been pretty bad, too. So it hasn't been easy for her at all, never mind putting up with the miserable work of the negotiations.

"It was soon after we had your peer counseling advisor workshop. She came away from one negotiating meeting that had been even worse than usual. At one point she said something to the superintendent about trying to reach some sort of compromise, and I guess he just lit into her and blasted her in front of everybody. But she kept her cool, somehow, and managed not to lose it for the rest of the meeting, but she was fighting back tears the whole time.

"The next day other members of the team complimented her on handling the superintendent's tirade the way she had and really praised her for not blowing up and creating a scene. I heard them and decided I would do something more tangible to let her know how I felt.

"So I went and got one of my little brown bear stickers and when I found her, I stuck it on the collar of her jacket. I told her that this was my way of telling her how much I appreciated all she was doing for us. I told her about the history of the bear programs.

"And then I said, 'You represented all of us. You bore the brunt of it all, and I want you to remember every time you look at the bear, that you are loved and respected by all of us. Wear it all day, so that you won't forget.'

"Do you know what she did? She wore the sticker all day and right into the negotiation meeting that afternoon. She showed it to everybody in the room, including the superintendent. Then she told everyone that her bear had a story. Wearing the bear was her way of saying that she knew she had support from other members of the faculty, and it helped her to remember that she was not alone in how she felt about the stalled negotiations and her intense desire to seek a compromise.

"The superintendent didn't say a word, and the team moved on—toward their compromise."

Chapter 14

Bear Power

Other stories surface as a result of using the bear stickers in the advisor workshop.

Arlington High School art teacher Pauline Finberg, a member of the MPHA Board of Directors, leaves the workshop deeply moved by the verbal feedback activity.

How amazing that an inexpensive stationery store sticker can become such a powerful tool in enhancing our human relationships! How strange that we shy away from telling people that they have made a difference—large or small—to us! How remarkable—the difficult, sometimes impossible task of sharing our loving thoughts and feelings with other people becomes a simple act—nothing more than fixing a tiny symbol on a collar or shirt pocket. Words come easily for a brief explanation, and a caring human exchange is completed.

Pauline thinks about her remaining stickers on the way home from the workshop. An exciting stream of possibilities runs through her mind.

When I think about it, I could be giving bear stickers away to so many people, all the time. We don't just all live or work together—we change each others' lives by what we do with them or for them. Maybe it's not true in every single instance, but I can think of plenty of people who have made a difference in my life—family, friends, teachers, and the students too. So where do I start?

Describing Pauline as an art teacher is like describing one small part of an intricately woven tapestry. She leads a very successful peer program, a support group for students who are grieving or have family and friends who are seriously ill, or who are ill themselves. She teaches, she designs, she paints, she writes, she coaches the cheerleading team, she pitches in when needed to help out in other departments, she counsels, consoles and comforts students and teachers alike.

She is also the faculty advisor to the Student Council.

Sean is a senior. He has been the president of the Student Council this year, following three years of work on the Council as an underclassman. He has been an outstanding president, never seeking the limelight, quietly carrying out all of his responsibilities, and many times picking up on small details that no one else can do because they "have no time". He delegates tasks appropriately and remembers to write thank you notes when the tasks are completed.

He has changed much of the usual effort and hard work of advising the Council into a pleasurable experience. Pauline decides that one of her bear stickers must go to Sean.

She finds him, explains about the bears and their history in peer helping, and about the stickers she had been given in the workshop.

"Sean, I don't want you to graduate and leave Arlington High School without telling you what a difference you have made in my life, particularly this year. You've been a joy to work with; you've made my job so much easier. I want you to wear this sticker all day, and remember when you look at it, that you are a very special person. And I hope you will remember that *I* won't forget all that you have done for me."

A proud Sean goes home wearing his symbol of specialness on his shirt collar. He tells his parents. He tells the rest of his family.

He goes off to college in the Fall to become a student leader there, active in sports, active in the student life of the school.

On coming home for the first time, he still talks about the bear to his family and what it means to him to have been recognized in such a personal way.

A return visit to school to visit with friends and faculty includes a stop in Pauline's art room.

"I don't have a bear to give you, but I do want you to know how often I have thought of you, and how much it meant to me to be given that little bear sticker. So I thought maybe giving you this little gift would come close to letting you know what a difference you made in my life, and now I'm thanking you for that."

It is a little angel figurine.

Chapter 14

Ask E. Willabee

In the meantime, back at Dover Sherborn, E. Willabee continues making the rounds. Remnants of scepticism surface only rarely and are put to rest quickly by the group and by the tales they tell of his reception when presented to the "bearees." On the other hand, from time to time it has been necessary to review and restate the purpose of our concept of the bear in order to prevent any inappropriate mysticism from developing.

He is not immortal.

He is not a "lucky penny" or a rabbit's foot.

He is not a miracle worker.

He cannot mend broken bones or cure illness.

He cannot ward off danger or survive extraordinary damage from external forces.

He is a Teddy Bear.

He is a warm and fuzzy symbol of the Peer Counseling group, a reminder that they think deeply and are concerned about other people, their joys and sorrows, successes and failures.

One time he needs emergency repairs because a curious family dog has decided he looks quite appetizing. Another time he needs replacement because while riding in the recipient's car, it is smashed in a freak accident and he is destroyed along with the car. At other times, he has been simply lost, perhaps buried in a crammed locker, perhaps smuggled away by a younger uninformed sibling.

He is as vulnerable to problems and stress as are his temporary owners.

"Love is supposed to wear out your fur a little," says the poster on my wall (Canard, 1994).

It doesn't matter. The means are developed for finding replacements or substitutions.

Naturally, intense discussions ensue after each of these instances and one thing often leads to another. As usual, once launched into the issue, they need no help from me or my co-advisor, Thom Hughart.

"We keep needing new bears. How often can we do this? Do we have a bear budget?"

"Or, ho, ho, only a *bare* budget?"

"Oh, yuck. Leave it to you, Bill. So, do you have any *real* ideas?"

"Look, we can't stop accidents from happening to him."

"No more than we can stop them from happening to ourselves or other people. Have you noticed?"

"Well, if I haven't learned anything else in this group, I've learned that we don't have all the answers to everything and can't solve everybody else's problems. I guess that includes not preventing all accidents and problems from happening in the first place."

"Hey, wait, though. We *have* learned *about* problem solving. What about the idea we mentioned a long time ago about a column in the school newspaper that addresses kids' problems, sort of like 'Ask Beth' or one of the other pieces in the big newspapers?"

"Oh, right. I remember talking about that. I wouldn't even mind doing some of the writing as long as it was stuff we worked on here in class."

"Where would we start? I wouldn't feel right about using things brought here in confidence."

"I wonder if we could get other kids to submit problems somehow—anonymously, I mean."

"Well, could we maybe put a box in the library or someplace else—you know—where everybody goes one time or another, and have kids put stuff in there?"

"Hey, yeah. Then we could collect the notes every week or so, really brain storm them here in class, and give sort of an outline of our ideas to Rachel or whoever else is going to write the article. That might work, at least eventually."

"Not bad. All the brainstorming will help all of us, too. Give us ideas we can use for working with similar issues with some of the kids assigned to us."

"Or not assigned to us. Like things that come up with friends and family all the time."

"What if nobody submits any problems? That could happen, you know."

"In a pinch, couldn't we use some of the problems that do get into the syndicated mail bags? We wouldn't need to quote them or anything—just pick up on the problems that are sent in."

"Hey, I know. We could call the column 'Ask E. Willabee!' How about that?"

"I like it! I like it! Let's do it."

Many of the difficulties the group have anticipated do arise. The "suggestion" or problem box rarely reveals other student issues. It needs what many peer helping activities or projects need—time for everyone to think about revealing a personal issue, even to an anonymous box, time to take the necessary risk of writing down such an issue, time to consider the trustworthiness of the peer counseling group, or their ability to help.

That too doesn't matter. Armed with problems submitted by teens nationwide on a daily basis to the "Dear Abby" or "Ask Beth" columns, they brainstorm, debate options, analyze possible consequences, and write their columns.

The first column introduces the concept to student and faculty readers, and goes on to address a topic of frequent discussion in the group meetings.

"'Ask E. Willabee: You Can Help'

by Rachel Derian

"'Ask E. Willabee' is a column created to address pertinent issues of Dover-Sherborn students and faculty. There will be a box in the library (near the personal box) where students and faculty may drop off questions, issues, thoughts, problems, etc., that they would like to see the Peer Counselors address.

"During the month of September, many Peer Counseling meetings have centered around the issue of drinking. What was once thought to be a social activity has become a problem at many of the upper classmen parties. Teenagers are no longer drinking to be social; many are drinking to get totally wasted, using alcohol to anesthetize themselves, for what reasons it's not always clear.

"We thought one reason for drinking to excess is to receive the attention that goes along with it. Girls often flock around another girl who is very drunk, for example. By giving a person attention when he or she is drunk, students unintentionally reinforce the self-abusive behavior. One alternative may be to talk to the person who seems to be drinking too much when he or she is sober. Then he or she will see that people reach out at other times besides when he or she is drinking.

"How to distinguish someone who is drinking too much from a social drinker? If the person is drunk at every party he or she attends, if the person can't enjoy a party unless there is alcohol, if a person needs a drink to be comfortable, that person is probably a problem drinker.

"The Peer Counselors are not experts. Alcoholics Anonymous, an organization that helps people help themselves, runs many meetings in the D-S area. You do not have to be an alcoholic to attend their meetings. On Wednesday nights at 8:00, there is an AA meeting at the Dover Catholic Church. On Thursday nights there is a meeting in the Kraft Hall of the Dover Church. Both meetings are open and relaxed. We suggest going because the meetings are informative. Also, Alcoholics Anonymous will send out schedules of all meetings in the area if called."

Some time later, E. Willabee puts hard problems aside, and addresses the issue of enhancing personal relationships:

Ask E. Willabee

"The Christmas season is upon us, and the Peer Counselors are noticing a change in everyone's behavior. It appears that the spirit of the holidays is starting to spread. What is it that makes this time of the year so special? Well, for one thing, people start to think positively of each other and appreciate those that are closest. Gift-giving symbolizes the gratitude we feel toward someone special in our lives.

"But Christmas isn't the only time of year that we can appreciate people. Friends deserve positive attention all year long. It may be easier to give a person a present at Christmas than to tell that person you care any time, but which one means more? Maybe our friendships would be more satisfying if verbal appreciation were shown. Often the people who complain that their 'friends' are fake are the ones who have a hard time communicating in a positive way with other people. Sarcasm and biting humor may pass the time, but neither is a basis for a relationship.

"Things that brighten up a day:
1. a happy smile
2. a laugh at a good joke
3. a hug
4. a compliment
5. to be asked 'how are you?'
6. a warm hello
7. a genuine listener

"Presents are great to receive, but warm people are more valued as friends than as gift-givers. Happy Holidays!"

Rachel Derian

Chapter 15

At Home and Around Town

It is not possible for any of us who are involved in bear activity in peer counseling programs at school to ignore our own family issues and the comfort made possible by the presence (or presents) of bears to troubled individuals or the joy of quiet recognition for those who have accomplished major or minor successes. For many of us, the gift of bears have become traditional for many occasions, and they have been accepted with the full understanding of the meaning behind their presentation and its relationship to the Peer Counseling program.

White bears of almost any size have become "the" appropriate baby or baby shower gift, First Communion gift, engagement gift, a sharing of the celebration.

Brown, black, beige, or two-tone large bears are often gifts of recognition and appreciation for jobs well done, for keynoters, committee chairs, or other help given by individuals for our annual MPHA conferences or other events.

Small brown or beige bears are end-of-the-year tokens of hard work done by graduate student interns in their school guidance practicum programs.

The same small bears, dressed or adorned for the particular occasion, have become the regular gift for friends or family in the hospital.

It is September of 1996. Our six children, their wives, husbands and children give us a major party in celebration of our fiftieth wedding anniversary. Old friends and new friends arrive from far and near. On top of our "wedding" cake the traditional couple is perched. Not so traditional is that they are two tiny jointed bears, made by our oldest daughter, Judy (yes, another bear maker). The Papa bear carries a basket of tiny woodworking tools. The Mama bear carries a basket of veggies from her garden.

My husband has to undergo bypass surgery in 1989. His bear is dressed in a doctor's green surgical gown. He (my husband, not the bear) recovers quickly, soon feeling better than he has in many months.

Chet Kennedy, a member of our MPHA Board of Directors, becomes very ill. Surgery is required, with a long convalescence following. His small white bear is dressed in nothing but a large band-aid. He travels to and from the hospital with Chet as he is readmitted periodically for treatments.

Five years later, my husband develops other serious health problems. More hospital admissions and more surgery. As I come into his hospital room the day after one surgical procedure, he says, "You haven't brought my bear in yet."

I bring in his bear.

He had worked hard at the 1993 Seventh Annual NPHA Conference at MIT, as had all of the people who worked on the Steering Committee. I had given him and each of the others a small bear as a token of appreciation. I bring that bear in to him.

That makes two.

Two days later, as I am making my way through the hospital corridor toward Cranny's room, there is Chet, in his hospital bathrobe, headed in the same direction. He is being discharged that day and is on his way to deliver *his* bear to Cranny.

That makes three.

The following day I come to the hospital for my visit to find that the Peer Counselors at the school where I am helping with the training have decided that *their* bear should go to him for the week. Their school guidance counselor (and peer counseling advisor) has brought him in.

That makes four.

The fourth bear goes back to the Peer Counseling group when the prescribed time is up. The other three come home with him, where they perch, long after his recovery, on the top of his chest of drawers.

They do not always stay in place, however.

One granddaughter, Missy, develops mono. Cranny brings his bear to her.

Soon after, another granddaughter, Susie, injures her knee in an athletic event. Missy calls to check with her grandfather and delivers the bear to her cousin Susie.

Cranny has to be readmitted to the hospital for a brief time. Susie brings the bear back to him.

It seems totally appropriate for us to have family-and-friends bears. With luck, they may stay in place for a while. If other problems develop, we know they will be welcomed wherever we send them.

Educational Media Corporation®

Chapter 16

The World Wide Bear Web

This isn't stopping here.

Now, as I search my memory and records for bear stories and talk to other people in the peer helping and Teddy Bear businesses, I discover extensive activities of which I have been only minimally aware. Teddy Bears have been a symbol of love and caring since they were first designed and marketed. There is evidence worldwide that young peer helpers are not alone in using the warm fuzziness of bears as a comforting presence in stressful times.

Those who watched the memorial services for the victims of the horrible Oklahoma City bombing saw grief-stricken family members holding bears sent to them from someone who believes that a Teddy Bear can bring some small comfort to persons in pain.

The "P.J. Huggabee" Teddy Bears, created by Marshall Field's for the "Help Me Grow" program partnership between Ronald McDonald's Children's Charities and the State of Illinois, were designed originally to give children taken into protective custody a "sense of security and companionship" (URL, 1995). The bears were sent to Oklahoma by Illinois' First Lady Brenda Edgar on behalf of the people of Illinois.

On the day of the bombing, cartoon artist Dan Wasserman of the *Boston Globe* sketched a grieving Teddy Bear with one paw covering his eyes, his sadness symbolizing the shock and sorrow of the entire country. Arrangements were made with the Los Angeles Times Syndicate to send copies of the drawing to anyone who donated money to the Victims and Families Relief fund in Oklahoma City. In a very short time, over $15,000 dollars were raised for the Fund.

As of September, 1995, at least three other states had launched P.J. Huggabee Bear programs—Minnesota, Wisconsin and Ohio.

The *Teddy Bear Review* reports that bears nationwide are being given to young hospitalized burn patients through the generosity of the "Burn Bear" program of the National Burn Victim Foundation. They were the inspiration of its president and founder, Harry J. Gaynor of Orange, New Jersey, and have been giving comfort to the young burn patients since June of 1992 (Cohen, 1996).

The Foundation says that as of July 1, 1996, over 5,900 Burn Bears have found homes with young burn victims throughout New Jersey, New York, Pennsylvania, Connecticut, Massachusetts, Ohio, Virginia, Florida, Illinois, Washington (state), Colorado, California and many others. "Wherever these bears have roamed, and wherever they continue to go, a smile on a suffering child's face always follows" (Such, 1996).

The Teddy Bear Artists' Association has developed a similar informal use of their own creations to send comfort to their own members. They rally to the news of members having a difficult time, often designing and sending special bears to suit a special need. One bear artist who had suffered the loss of her husband was the recipient of a bear a day, each from a different fellow artist during the critical holiday season.

One bear designer, now semi-retired, limits her creation and production to special bears for handicapped or disabled children. Her Teddy Bears imitate the disability and give each child a comforting friend who is "just like me." All of these bears are donated to the children.

Good Bears of the World is an organization that was founded in 1969 by James T. Ownby. Its members "come from all walks of life and share an interest in giving comfort in a quiet, low-key fashion." Their aim is to place "the comfort of a Teddy Bear into the arms and hearts of every traumatized child or lonely, forgotten adult in the world." The James T. Ownby Memorial Bear Bank was created to enable Good Bears of the World to have available a constant supply of bears to fill the requests that come to them every day from nursing homes, crisis and abuse centers, police and fire departments, hospitals, hospices, and other human services agencies, all of whom use Teddies to help comfort those who are frightened or in emotional or physical pain (What GBW, 1996).

In an issue of *Bear Tracks* (1996), Linda Mullins describes the Berryman's International Teddy Bear Artists Auction, which was held in Tokyo soon after the terrible earthquake at Kobe. They raised nearly $220,000 for the Japanese Society of Pediatric Psychiatric, to aid them in their work with the thousands of devastated children.

In that same issue of *Bear Tracks,* we are told that The Celestial Seasonings Tea Company has funded a "Buddy Bear" program since 1985. They started with a donation of 40 bears to the Boulder Police Department, then escalated to over 4,000 bears within three years to fire and police departments, ambulance and paramedical teams, victim witness programs, and other public health agencies, all in the state of Colorado (Good Bears, Spring, 1996).

BEARS & BAUBLES, of Albany, New York, a Good Bears of the World Store Sponsor, donated two dozen bears to the Albany police and fire departments.

In the towns of Amherst and in Leominster, Massachusetts, police cruisers carry Teddy Bears with them to comfort children who might be present in cases of domestic violence or other traumatic situations. In Leominster, bears are also available in the police station for children who might be brought there in similar circumstances. They are donated by the local Rotary, but the Leominster Police also keep bear badges and bear lollipops as additional supports for these times.

Educational Media Corporation®

Students from Mt. Vernon High School, Mt. Vernon, NY, have formed the Mt. Vernon Teen Task Force on AIDS. They work with AIDS victims in New York City and bring bears to patients, some of them children. The bears were donated by Karen Shirey, a Good Bears of the World member. Shirey also donated two dozen GBW bears to the youth groups of the Toby Valley and Brockport Methodist Churches. The students in the Church Youth Groups take the bears to shut-ins in their communities (Henderson, Spring, 1996a).

In California, Attorney Ernestine Fields, concerned over the emotional state of young children brought into the Children's Courthouse of the Los Angeles Dependency Court, sought funds from friends, foundations, businesses and colleagues. She established and incorporated Comfort for Court Kids, which distributed 11,000 Teddy Bears in 1995. By January, 1996, the number had grown to 216 bears per week given to infants, toddlers, young children, and teenagers, to help them through the trauma of extreme family discord and the court processes that ensued (Henderson, Spring 1996b).

On December 19, 1993, in Wellesley, Massachusetts, Ann Greenawalt Abernethy, minister of the Wellesley Congregational Church, began her Christmas sermon with a discourse on Teddy Bears. She referred to an editorial from the *Boston Globe* entitled "West's Apology to Bosnia—Send in Teddy Bears." It discusses the frustrated helping attempts of the United Nations to alleviate the suffering in Bosnia (McGrory, 1993).

In her sermon, Abernethy (1993) says, "The world doesn't really know what to do about Bosnia. Rightly or wrongly, everyone so far has decided to leave them alone, hoping they'll come to their senses. The world's leaders and people are less and less sure whether violent interference from outside stops violence or escalates it. So, for now, we do what we can with humanitarian aid, including dropping Teddy Bears into the countryside. I wish all those perpetuating the killing in Bosnia would pick up a Teddy Bear this Christmas. Now that wish may seem naive and frivolous, but maybe, just maybe, a Teddy Bear could put them in touch with their playful-child hearts and the hearts of Bosnia's hurting children. And maybe, just maybe, a Teddy Bear could turn them around to see again life's wonder and preciousness and put a stop to their crazed behavior."

I am sometimes accused of being too simplistic in my views of the world. Perhaps it is true.

Some years ago in a fantasy exercise for a graduate school summer workshop on Peer Helping, I imagined a world with peer helping programs in every school, business, public and private institution—a world where love and respect and decency were the norm. A world delivered from evil and hate and greed. A world at peace, through love.

So, I am also an incurable optimist.

Perhaps there is hope for the ultimate realization of that fantasy.

And maybe, just maybe, small Teddy Bears can be one of the tools for helping us to make it happen.

References

Abernethy, A.G. (1993, December 19). King of hearts. Wellesley, MA: The Wellesley Congregational Church.

Bridges, H. (1993). Who you are makes a difference. In *Chicken soup for the soul,* Canfield & Hansen (Eds.). Deerfield Beach, FL: Health Communications, pp. 19-21.

Canard, L. (1994). *All I need to know about life I learned from my Teddy Bear.* Corte Madera, CA: Portal Publications, LTD.

Cohen, J.H. (1996, May/June). The salve of human kindness. *Teddy Bear Review,* pp. 66-68.

Cranshaw, F. & Hughart, T. (1979). *Peer counseling: a program in caring* [Slide tape/video]. Dover, MA.

Good Bears enter Best Buddy program in Colorado. (1996, Spring). *Bear Tracks: Journal of the Good Bears of the World,* p 24.

Henderson, S. (1996, Spring a). Very short stories. *Bear Tracks: Journal of the Good Bears of the World,* pp. 20-21.

Henderson, S. (1996, Spring b). Weekly need: 18 dozen bears! *Bear Tracks: Journal of the Good Bears of the World,* p. 25.

McGrory, M. (1993, November 27). West's apology to Bosnia—send in Teddy Bears. *The Boston Globe,* p. 11.

Mullins, L. (1996, Spring). GBW was there when artist bears raised nearly $220,000 in Tokyo. *Bear Tracks: Journal of the Good Bears of the World, p. 12.*

Sturkie, J. (1987). *Listening with love: True stories from peer counseling.* San Jose, CA: Resource Publications, pp. 22-27.

Such, J.M. (1996). The burn bear story. Basking Ridge, NJ: The National Burn Victim Foundation.

URL. (1995). http://www.state.ilus/Gov/pj.htm, November 1.

What GBW is all about. (1996, Summer). *Bear Tracks: Journal of the Good Bears of the World,* pp. 31-34.